Take What Resonates and Leave What Doesn't

Amanda Croker

Presentation by *BookLeaf Publishing*

Web: www.bookleafpub.com

E-mail: info@bookleafpub.com

ISBN: 9789357618519

First edition 2023

DEDICATION

For my two greatest accomplishments in life, my sons Riley and Chayce. May you always dream big and no matter your age follow those dreams, chase them until you catch them and once you do….. dream some more.

Loving you always and endlessly, Mum.

ACKNOWLEDGEMENT

With love and gratitude,

To my amazing, selfless parents, Cyril and Kaylene Croker, all that I was, all that I have and all that I am - I owe to you both.

To my cherished friend and best steak griller on a bbq ever, Hank Read, for his unique ways of encouraging me to believe in myself more which gave me the courage to write this book.

To my friend and colleague Debi Lane, for being my sounding board and patiently dealing with my chaos for the 21 days of writing.

To my mate and the hardest working sheep shearer I know, Adam Willding, may we always remain smarter than your average bears throughout our friendship, even when we have caramel milkshake in our shoes.

And to BookLeaf publishing for the incredible opportunity to be part of this creative writing challenge.

PREFACE

Musings written in verse about yearning for the love and acceptance I freely gave away but never received. This mini collection only took me 21 days to write….. but 20 years to learn how to gift love and acceptance to myself.

I'm addicted to the written word, I believe through poetry and quotes we can change the world. I am only one person, I can not do it alone. If I reach just one person, one is all that's needed, in turn, that one person will go on to reach another one and so on and so on - thus the ripple effect will grow in numbers.

By sharing snippets of my personal struggles on this journey, if my words bring comfort, hope, or solace to even just one person, then I've succeeded.

May you take what resonates and leave what doesn't.

Fear vs Thoughts

Too shy to be myself,
For the fear of being noticed,
Too empathetic to break another's heart,
For the fear of absorbing their pain.

Too sensitive to call others out,
For fear of facing their wrath,
Too proud to say 'I'm sorry',
For the fear of giving in.

Too curious to just sit back and watch,
For fear of missing out,
Too weak to show my strengths,
For the fear of being envied.

Too embarrassed to say what I feel,
For the fear of being mocked,
Too scared to do the wrong thing,
For the fear of punishment.

Too dreamy to live life in the moment,
For I fear my own reality,
Too emotionally profound to be in love,
For fear of rejection.

Too preoccupied with my health,
For the fear of ailing sickness,
Too cowardly to be brave,
For I have the fear of failing.

But...... to sit and write these words,
I have no fear of thoughts.....

The Art of Loving

The sweetest joy a soul can know,
The saddest weight a heart can bear,
The pinnacle of ecstasy,
And the valley of despair.

The sharpest knife that ever cut,
The healing spirit unparalleled,
The burning desire just to touch,
And the deepest need to be held.

Peals of laughter ringing out,
A well of tears unshed,
Like running into a blazing fire,
A waiting heart that bled.

The suffering torment of rejection,
And hot relief of returned emotion,
Angry words and hasty actions,
The softest whispers and tender passion.

The Power of a Kiss

The successful art of kissing,
Is telling a story using no words,
An expression of raw vulnerability,
Allowing your innermost desires to be heard.

A kiss can be playful and fun,
Lightly planted all over your lover's face,
Nibbling their lips, teasing with your tongue,
Slow, fast or both, your kiss can set the pace.

A kiss drenched in passion and longing,
You stand locked lip to lip,
Bodies pressed close together,
Embracing each other hip to hip.

A kiss so utterly intense,
Nerve endings tingle and it takes your breath away,
A kiss of savage urgency,
Animalistic hunger, begging them to stay.

A kiss so delicately tentative,
Enticing you to take the lead,
To show them they are wanted,
To show them you've heard their need.

If you love someone special,
Do not underestimate the power of a kiss,
For it is telling you things,
That, trust me, you do not want to miss.

The Key

I had closed the door upon my heart,
And I wouldn't let anyone in,
I had trusted and loved only to be hurt.
But swore it would never happen again.

I had locked the door and tossed the key,
As hard and as far as I could,
Love would never enter there again,
My heart was closed for good.

Then you came into my life
And made me change my mind,
Just when I thought that the key,
Was virtually impossible to find.

That's when you held out your arm,
Proving to me that I was wrong,
Inside the palm of your hand laid the key to my heart,
Astonishingly, you had it all along.

Rainbows

When you look into my eyes,
I feel as though you're reading my mind,
You discovered something within me,
I believed no one would ever find.

You took my heart into your hands,
And gently held it until it beat steady,
Because of you I am no longer afraid,
With you I know I am ready.

It is with you that I will triumph,
Any obstacles I may face,
No longer lost and lonely in life,
Standing beside you is my correct place.

United with you it's easier to bear,
All my past sorrow and pain,
You're the one who has taught me,
About rainbows after the downpours of rain.

Confusion

I'm sitting here trying to put an end,
To all the confusion swirling in my head,
Searching for answers to some questions,
Because his actions don't match what he said.

I want to know does he see a future with me,
I need to know what his intentions with me are,
I want to know when he's looking into my eyes,
Is he seeing my galaxy of stars?

Does he see how I'm unique?
Does he believe he is worthy of me?
Is he a man of action and willing to step up,
If those answers are: no, not quite or maybe?

Perhaps it's no more than merely a fun time,
I simply have pretty eyes for looking at,
Casual friends, no more no less,
Except in certain moments, he makes sure
I don't feel like that.

My fondness for him runs deep,
Deeper than any ocean or sea
I ponder over the love he's willing to give,
But 90% of me knows he won't share it with me.

The remaining 10% is drowning in faith and hope,
It's what keeps me treading waters with him,
The not knowing and always trying to guess,
Leaves me uncertain if I will sink or swim.

Breadcrumbs and Booty Calls

I was starving for commitment and love,
But settled for breadcrumbs and booty calls,
Yet the reason for my insistent hunger eluded me,
As shame and disgust encased me like four walls.

For every night I cried myself to sleep,
A fortress was built around my heart one brick at a time,
Vowing not to grant anyone access through it,
While desperately wishing someone would climb.

That rather than being admired for my strength,
Or being told I want too much and I'm far too deep,
The one worthy of all I had to offer and give,
Would see beyond the wounds, knowing I was someone he
wanted to keep.

He would see the fortress for what it was,
A means to protect what precious little was left,
With him, there wouldn't be a need for it,
As he would willingly provide a safe space for me to rest.

Eventually, I detached my emotions from my reality,
I don't know exactly when that occurred,
It just so happened that one day I realised,
Loving someone in my daydreams was what I preferred.

Part of my soul craves a villain's dark kiss,
For it offers me something taboo and forbidden,
I have tasted it twice but each time he's left,
Forcing my own demon to remain hidden.

I knew it wasn't helpful or healthy,
To live in the fantasies of my mind,
But for the longest time that's where I remained,
Waiting in the perfect spot for him to come and find.

Self Abandoning

Sacrificing my own needs,
Endeavouring to sate another's desire,
Seeking out forever in temporary people,
I got burnt every time by the fire.

Fuelled by the belief if I could cater,
To their every want and need,
There'd be no reason for my armour,
As my heart wouldn't break and bleed.

Such foolish notions filled my head,
For years and years and years,
That love was simply always enough,
To conquer anyone's fears.

Numerous harsh lessons were learned,
Many bitter pills indeed were swallowed,
Throughout my quest of finding love,
On the road less travelled that I followed.

One day it finally dawned on me,
The reason everything always went wrong,
You can not make someone appreciate,
What they've never valued all along.

Your Ghost

Another day of work is done,
Set the alarm and lock the door on my way out,
I go through the motions feeling numb,
No more tears fall, for my eyes are in drought.

Rivers of tears have already been shed,
Unanswered begging has been pleaded to above,
Brought to my knees and broken,
All my senses fraught from neglect and lost love.

All your things are gone, the spaces left behind still
bare,
This house once vibrant and shared as a home,
Is now half empty and eerily silent,
The place I should feel loved but where I feel most
alone.

My mind is haunted with images of you,
And how our life used to be,
My heart feels trapped in a cage,
Like a blackbird longing to be free.

I fear this hollowness has set in for good,
Even though forgetting you is what I want most,
I resign to pouring myself a glass of wine,
Playing our song and dancing with your ghost.

Photographs

Sepia coloured and cherished,
A moment in time to capture,
Forever etched into the paper,
Ink stains to leave you in rapture.

Memories to remind us,
The faces of loved ones passed,
The experiences shared,
Showing us good nor bad times last.

A way to trip down memory lane,
When our own minds seem to fail,
To reminisce about the times,
Life was perfect and there was no need to bail.

Display them on the mantle or hide them in a drawer,
Display them on the fridge or even on the wall,
Proud moments, happy days, even sad ones too,
Take as many as you can, please just photograph it
all.

Legacy

A little mad, mysterious and moody,
I was never one to seek out popularity,
I'm brave enough to love the whole world,
And empty enough to embrace its cruelest
barbarity.

A slave to my emotions,
My heart is a graveyard like ancient ruins,
With logic and rationality failing,
To rid me of my unwavering delusions.

We live in a world of modern conveniences,
Instant gratification and quick fixes,
Yet I still hope for old-fashioned chivalry,
Courtship, honour and dragon-slaying princes.

Perhaps my purpose is just to give love,
There's oceans of it flowing inside of me,
As much as I yearn to receive it,
Maybe the love I give will be my legacy.

The Beach

The heat of the sun warms my skin,
The cool breeze dances through my hair,
The instability of sand shifts under my feet,
With the aroma of salt wafting in the air.

I walk for a while along the edge,
Away from everyone so I can be alone,
I sit, close my eyes and meditate,
Then steal a glance at you before collecting shells
and a heart-shaped stone.

You raised your arms and bent your knees,
A gentle jump as your feet left the ocean floor,
The sunshine glistened off the curve of your back,
As you dove into a wave crashing onto the shore.

Afterwards we sat together on the rocks,
Both rejuvenated in our own individual ways,
While you spoke of your refreshing swim,
I wished that it was the way we would forever stay.

The way you looked at me and smiled,
Felt like heaven on earth was within reach,
We didn't hold hands as we walked,
But I'll never forget that day at the beach.

Profound

To feel everything profoundly,
Is it a blessing or a curse?
Truth is at different times, it's both,
And there'll be days you won't know what's worse.

To feel all things in extremes,
So deeply it penetrates your core,
The stinging heat of flames,
As they lick and singe your door.

As they begin to engulf your flesh,
You know you'll be consumed by the fire,
Yet you also know that from the ashes you will rise,
So no situation is ever truly dire.

For the depth of which you feel,
Every ounce of sorrow and pain,
Is matched by your ability,
To withstand the storm and rain.

For even when skies are grey,
You find beauty in all that you see,
Because you feel love, happiness and joy,
Just as extreme and just as profoundly.

Life's Battles

Life could get so hard,
That at times I wanted to die,
Then I thought of all I love,
And I wondered why?

Why do I feel this way,
When life holds treasures for me?
Because in life's darkest moments,
It's all those treasures I could not see.

Life's battles will vary from petty to drastic,
Many you'll overcome with relative ease,
Others can take a little more time and effort,
Then there's the incessant ones that just won't leave..

Awareness has opened my eyes,
I'm finally thinking straight,
When I look at life now,
I choose happiness instead of hate.

I hope these humble words can help,
All of those who have ever felt the same,
To realise that perspective is what matters,
If you want to win at life's game.

Comfortably Numb

No one consciously chooses it,
A world of darkness to spend your days,
In the beginning you don't even notice,
Until one day you find yourself trapped in the maze.

You steel your resolve to fight it,
You swear you'll do whatever it takes to resist,
But it gets exhausting to battle your own mind,
Your fears and emotions just feed the abyss.

So you stop trying to find a way out,
Allowing it to devour you without defences,
At the thought of risking your heart,
You protect the organ and lose one of your senses.

You discover you can still see fuzzy shapes,
As your eyes adjust to the black void,
You rely on other senses to guide your way,
And pretend your essence wasn't carelessly destroyed.

You convince yourself that dark is safe,
Time passes and you stop craving the light,
Outside forces offer help and support,
But the sunshine they want to bring in is just too bright.

Their helpful mantra - love the light,
Hate the dark and fear shadows of grey,
Colours have no differences when you're
comfortably numb,
No one understands that, no matter what you say.

The magic I found being in darkness saved me,
It's the cornerstone of my self-reflection and healing,
It provided me understanding, forgiveness and peace,
These insightful gifts helped me welcome back
feelings.

Every single person has a shadow self,
Do not ignore the darkness that resides within,
There is no need to fear, dismiss nor hate it,
Once you accept and love it, that's when your life
will truly begin.

Confidence

When your mind is in one place,
While your heart is in another,
Confusion is born, giving rise to doubts,
And 'what ifs' that threaten to smother.

Best not to romanticise,
What could be or might've been,
Respect and value yourself enough.
To believe what your eyes have seen.

For people will always show you,
Just exactly who they are,
Be courageous enough to look,
Or wind up with another unhealed scar.

The journey from your heart to your head,
Is said to be the hardest one to make,
But like the true north of a compass,
Your soul knows the way and what turns to take.

So trust in the universe divine,
Raise your vibration and soar,
Express gratitude for opportunities presented,
As you confidently walk through every door.

2 Dates and a Dash

Everything comes at a price,
Everything has a risk,
To live a life without regret,
One must ask themselves this.

What is it I want the most,
In the life I dream about?
What are the things I do not need?
What is it I can not live without?

Focus not on what others say,
Nor what they say you must do,
Accountability is heavy to carry,
And the responsibility falls on you.

Speak your words with conviction,
Commit your actions with intention,
If something gives you the heebee jeebees,
It means it doesn't deserve your attention.

Ultimately life is just 2 dates and a dash,
You'll realise when your time comes to pass,
Make sure your final trip down memory lane,
Is full of wonder, love and laughs.

Into the Woods

The air is thick, my thoughts are muddled,
My limbs feel sluggish and slow,
Mother Nature calls my name,
So into the woods I go.

To feel the grass and touch the dirt,
And begin to recharge my soul,
I must realign and reconnect,
So my spirit and body are whole.

As leaves on the trees gently rustle,
Alone in the forest I feel free,
To take a deep breath and exhale,
Releasing the troubles that are weighing on me.

No planning, no thinking, no stress,
For in here I don't have to worry,
Time stands still while I seek peace of mind,
The world outside is forgotten in a hurry.

So if you see me distracted and restless,
Please suggest a trip into the woods,
I'd be humbly delighted and grateful,
To finally be seen and understood.

Adventure

It could be bravery or madness,
In all honesty, who really knows,
Come along for a crazy ride,
No destination, just see how far it goes.

We'll let the universe provide opportunities,
We'll broaden our horizons saying yes instead of
no,
Stepping out of our comfort zones,
Is after all, the only way to grow.

Adventure awaits us in the wind,
There's a big old world beyond this town,
Full of strangers who will become our friends,
And a trove of treasures to be found.

I've made my decision, my bags are packed,
I've only got one thing left to do,
Ask you, throw caution to the wind and join me,
I know this journey would be sweeter with you.

War Must Cease

Centuries ago war was the solution,
According to some gallant knights and a king,
All these years later with hindsight of errors,
Alas, we still have not learned a single thing.

War must cease,
Before all life ceases,
For if we can't live in peace,
We shall die in pieces.

Egotistical greed is the driving force,
Behind unrestrained use of arbitrary power,
Weaponry and attacks deployed and unleashed,
Blanketing whole cities in their darkest hour.

An eye for an eye, a tooth for a tooth,
Makes the world a bitter place,
We must implement compassion and kindness,
To restore faith and humanity in our race.